I0839109

SELF-CONFIDENCE

A 21-Day Challenge to Develop Confidence,
Overcome Limiting Beliefs,
Become Irresistible
& Courageous

Wallace Foulds

Text Copyright © 2018 Wallace Foulds

All rights reserved. No part of this guide may be reproduced in any form without permission in writing from the publisher except in the case of brief quotations embodied in critical articles or reviews.

Legal & Disclaimer

The information contained in this book is not designed to replace or take the place of any form of medicine or professional medical advice. The information in this book has been provided for educational and entertainment purposes only.

The information contained in this book has been compiled from sources deemed reliable, and it is accurate to the best of the Author's knowledge; however, the Author cannot guarantee its accuracy and validity and cannot be held liable for any errors or omissions. Changes are periodically made to this book. You must consult your doctor or get professional medical advice before using any of the suggested remedies, techniques, or information in this book.

Upon using the information contained in this book, you agree to hold harmless the Author from and against any damages, costs, and expenses, including any legal fees potentially resulting from the application of any of the information provided by this guide. This disclaimer applies to any damages or injury caused by the use and application, whether directly or indirectly, of any advice or information presented, whether for breach of contract, tort, negligence, personal injury, criminal intent, or under any other cause of action.

You agree to accept all risks of using the information presented inside this book. You need to consult a professional medical practitioner in order to ensure you are both able and healthy enough to participate in this program.

CONTENTS

INTRODUCTION

With confidence, you can take on the world. It is potent. It is essential. Yet, it is in short supply.

A lack of confidence comes in many forms, and self-doubt often hides behind a façade of what looks like self-confidence and assuredness, but it is only a show.

For many, even with success that others covet, they still feel undeserving of its rewards. For the rest, they never found success because they believed that their own voice would come across as deficient or self-important, so they never left their comfort zone; and therefore, they never challenged themselves or took risks.

For both types of people, potential is lost, and lost again, and again.

Have you been waiting for confidence to arrive, so that you can live a life doing things that matter? Have you accepted your lack of confidence as a part of you? In other words, have you owned it in order to feel better about your days and yourself?

How would your life change if you developed confidence that was genuine and bold? What could you do that you cannot do now? What opportunities would open up to you if you were just a bit more self-assured on a daily basis? What opportunities have already passed you by because of your lack of confidence? In all, what have you given away, hoping for a miracle that confidence would find you without any work involved?

Are there other ways to describe how you feel most of the time?

- Do you have self-doubt?

- Do you have performance anxiety?

- Do you have a fear of failure?

All of these things tie to a lack of self-confidence.

Most importantly, are your ambitions, hopes, and dreams hampered and on hold because of something in your belly that tells you to escape to the clear instead of face challenges that would propel you to new levels?

The ability to be self-assured is somewhere inside of you, but you are not able to follow your dreams because you do not know the rules of that tricky game called confidence. Clearly, self-confidence comes natural to some people and requires little effort on their part to display it, but for the rest of us, there are hurdles to negotiate and walls to dismantle before we find the freedom to pursue our goals with self-assuredness.

Over the course of 21 days, this book delivers a plan for you to gain self-confidence and keep it. The objective is to change the way you think by introducing you to the secret rules of self-confidence.

You will develop "psychological flexibility," which allows you to respond in a positive way to anxiety, fear, and self-doubt. Through the measures found in reading forward, you will improve your life physically, mentally, creatively, socially, and professionally. You will become a better parent and partner, a better employee and leader, and find new adventures and a higher quality of life.

Part One:
The Foundation

Day 1:
Self-Confidence Matters

"With realization of one's own potential and self-confidence in one's ability, one can build a better world."

Dalai Lama

There is a purpose behind your desire to be more confident. Therefore, you have to look beyond "confidence" to those things that have evaded you for years. You might not have a clear picture of what those desires and goals entail, so the first step is to fine-tune your notions of what added confidence will provide to you.

The first exercise is to answer the following questions. The answers to these questions should require significant thought, and a pen and paper, as well as a quiet place away from this book for a while. Write these questions down and really think about them:

> ➤ If you had as much self-confidence as you desire, how would you behave differently than you act now?

> ➤ If you had as much self-confidence as you desire, what sort of things would you do?

> ➤ If you had as much self-confidence as you desire, what sort of person would you become?

Now that you have your answers, below are some examples of real responses, according to Dr. Russ Harris, a psychotherapist, medical practitioner, and life coach, who wrote *The Confidence Gap*:

- A real estate agent wants to enroll at a university part-time, earn an MBA, and change careers

- A shy receptionist wants to be more outgoing, open, and talkative in her personal life and at the office, and join an online dating agency to meet new people

- An unemployed dancer wants to attend more auditions and dance better in front of judges

- A semi-professional tennis player wants to play better under pressure and win more matches as a result

- A shy scientist wants to be more genuine, warm, and engaging in social situations and make more friends

- A taxi driver wants to be intimate with his spouse after years of dealing with a "fear of failure"

- A junior manager wants to contribute more in meetings and give suggestions

- A mother of two wants to be assertive around her domineering mother

- A senior manager wants to be more effective at making decisions under pressure and be better at giving performance appraisals to his staff

- A restaurateur wants to take out a bank loan and open a restaurant at a second location

- An insurance claims processor wants to leave his marriage that is joyless and empty and start a new relationship

- A therapist wants to be more creative and start writing a novel

Now that you have other examples, you might want to fine-tune your first response as you answer more questions. Again, if you had unlimited confidence:

- How would you behave differently?

- How would your character change?

- How would you talk to yourself and treat yourself differently?

- What would you stop doing?

- What would you start doing?

- How would you perform differently at work and socially?

- How would you treat your spouse or partner, children, relatives, friends, and colleagues?

- What goals would you set out to accomplish?

- What difference would help make in the world?

Have a clear purpose on day one, as you head into the next three weeks of change. They are vital to your journey.

Day 2:
The Difference Between Goals and Values

"A goal properly set is halfway reached."

Zig Ziglar

It is important to understand the difference between values and goals. Values are ongoing actions that define you and how you want to act every day. You never think of values as being complete because they are an essential part of your constitution. In other words, if your values included loyalty, equality, and assertiveness, you would never "complete" those things, while goals can be finished out. Goals are desired outcomes that you achieve through a value-driven life. The moment you achieve the goal, you move onto the next one.

For more clarification, consider that you want to make good scores on your next work evaluation or school report. "Making a good score" is not a value; it is a goal. The value you would need to get that good score would be applying yourself at work or school, and dedicating yourself to being a more diligent worker and reducing inconsequential distractions. Here are some other examples of goals and values:

- Your goal is to lose ten pounds. Your value is to maintain and strengthen yourself physically.

- Your goal is to have more friends. Your value is to be friendly, outgoing, genuine, and supportive.

- Your goal is to buy a house in a safe neighborhood that has plenty of room for everyone. Your value is to protect and provide for your family.

- Your goal is to win a race or other sports competition. Your value is to train to the best of your ability, be competent in your daily preparation, and to be enthusiastic and energized during the contest.

We find ongoing fulfillment by upholding to our values and living them everyday with gusto, even when the journey to reach our goals takes months, years, or a decade.

For the task of Day 2, you will turn your answers from yesterday into complete statements in order to have a full grasp on the goals you wish to accomplish, and as you continue to read, we will provide the rules for how to accomplish them through value-driven confidence.

- I will act differently (<u>in these ways</u>).

- I will treat others differently (<u>in these ways</u>).

- I will treat myself differently (<u>in these ways</u>).

- I will develop (<u>these qualities and strengths</u>) and demonstrate (<u>these things</u>) to others.

- (<u>These are the ways</u>) I will behave differently with family and friends.

- (<u>These are the ways</u>) I will behave differently at work, school, or during activities.

> ➢ I will stand for (<u>these important things</u>).

> ➢ I will start doing (<u>these activities</u>).

> ➢ I will work towards (<u>these goals</u>).

> ➢ I will take (<u>these actions</u>) to improve my life.

After you complete the statements, keep this list with you wherever you go. Fine-tune it whenever it makes sense to do so. The statements may start as vague, but clarity will come, so update it often.

Day 3:
The Confidence Divide

"There can be no failure to a man who has not lost his courage, his character, his self-respect, or his self-confidence. He is still a King."

Orison Swett Marden

Let us get into the meat of the matter now that you have a better idea of what you want to accomplish. Answer this question: "Why does self-confidence even matter?" You might know the answer with no reservation, or you might not have a sound answer, though you know it is important. Your goals, which you have created, are a big part of the answer.

The bottom line is that you want a feeling of certainty and assurance wherever you go. You want to feel a powerful sense of ease that you can handle or adapt to any situation without pause. Confidence is also an act of trust. It is an unwavering feeling that you will be fine regardless of the outcome. You do not have to win every turn as long as your values are in check. Furthermore, the act, or the action of trust, will deliver you through until the feelings are actually present. You are not going to wake up and feel confident. Instead, you are going to practice confidence in all of its heat, and if you do it through your core beliefs, you will feel good in the end. Everyone must earn confidence, and you will find the reward of self-assurance one day if you do the work involved.

We are all confident in some of the things that we do, and it is probably because we have the experience and skill to do them.

SELF CONFIDENCE

We have practiced the task for so long that it has become a habit. Therefore, we do not feel any fear or have excessive expectations when performing the task, and we do not place harsh self-judgment upon ourselves before the task begins. Those things that we do not have confidence in doing fall into one of those categories below:

- Lack of skill preoccupies you

- Lack of experience preoccupies you

- Fear preoccupies you

- Excessive expectations preoccupy you

- Harsh self-judgment preoccupies you

Let us take a peek at each one of them separately, so you know exactly what you are facing when you are not feeling confident:

- You **lack skill** in a certain area; therefore, you are not confident about doing something. It is logical for you to be void of confidence when you attempt to do something you have not learned to do well yet.

- You **lack experience** in a certain area; therefore, you are not confident about doing something. Again, it is rational to have issues with confidence when you attempt to do something you never do, or do not do very often.

- You fear something and your **preoccupation with fear** cripples you. Fear comes in many forms. You might be afraid of things going badly and feeling rejection, embarrassment, or failing. You might even be worried about your overall reputation because rejection, embarrassment, or failure seems the likely route to destroyed stature or status. You do not want people to think you are a fool because you make a mistake, and you begin to think that trying it is a complete waste of time because of your preoccupation.

- However, fear is a thing that pops into the minds of the most awe-inspiring performers from the stage to the boardroom. You can have fear and be confident. The division comes when fear preoccupies you, and as it dwells, it festers, and destroys confidence.

- You have **excessive expectations** and you become obsessive with perfection. You dread making a mistake, and you are highly critical of yourself when you do not meet your own high standards. You quickly find fault through your less-than-perfect past experiences and you are now controlled by the notion that trying something is a waste of time because you cannot do it right; or at least, you cannot do it to your level of expectation.

- You **self-judge harshly**, which consistently undermines your attempts at confidence. You tell yourself that you are inadequate and incompetent, or you are unlikable and no good. You might even feel that you have gotten this far in life through luck and that you are a fraud, and soon, someone will expose you.

Now that you are aware of what might be separating you from self-confidence, there are four steps to bridging the divide:

Step 1: Practice the Skills. To become a confident public speaker, you have to practice speeches. If you want to be a confident writer, you have to practice writing. You cannot get around this reality.

The mental barriers that we just discussed keep us from practicing. Those walls manifest into lack of willpower and motivation, and thinking about the practice sessions can be draining because that is what fear and anxiety does to a person.

Step 2: Apply the Skills. Practicing is important, and effective application of practice is a necessity. This requires real life scenarios that are real challenging, in which you are presumably way outside of your comfort zone and faced with fear, anxiety, and self-doubt.

Focusing on the task is important in this scenario because you will not be able to do the task very well if you are absorbed in fear instead of the situation. Psychologists call it "task-focused attention" and Eastern gurus call it "mindfulness." Staying engaged and absorbing yourself in the task brings fulfillment.

Step 3: Reflect and Assess the Results. You need to analyze what worked and what did not, and use those notes to prepare for your next application of the skill. Your critique of yourself should reduce the amount of pressure you feel going into the task. You are testing yourself and finding the flaws in your approach. In other words, you are not looking to find perfection on the first go-around, or ever. Do not put that sort of pressure on yourself. You must be non-judgmental and self-encouraging. Improvement is your objective, but still, setbacks do happen, and you must allow for those as well.

Step 4: Modify the Practice and Application as Needed. Now, take your results and modify your approach and delivery. You should do more of the things that you do well, and improve upon the things that proved to be a weakness. You are developing and it is a beautiful thing that you are even at Step 4. When you are here, you should celebrate because you are systematically conquering your lack of confidence, and that should feel wonderful. Later in the book, we will give you tools to overcome the mental obstacles that might get to you in the first two steps.

You do a thousand things everyday with confidence. You know how to do this, and we will show you the rules, but for now, it is important that you acknowledge that work is involved from practice to application. In other words, today you appreciate that you need committed action as you proceed.

Also, consider that confidence is not a lack of fear. Everyone feels fear when he or she takes a risk outside of his or her comfort zone. It is a natural state. Fear is not any enemy to anyone. Fear is a friend that provides energy, which you can harness and use for your benefit. Fear does not hold people back; no, it is one's attitude towards fear that holds people back. Therefore, your task is to transform your relationship with fear. Later, we will guide you through this.

Day 4:
Acceptance and Commitment

"It takes a deep commitment to change and an even deeper commitment to grow."

Ralph Ellison

In the 1980s, Dr. Stephen Hayes developed ACT. He created the Acceptance and Commitment Therapy system to treat people with depression. The model worked for him and his patients, but it was so revolutionary it took 25 years before the psychology world embraced it enthusiastically. In fact, eventually, psychologists latched onto the concepts of ACT with such gusto that it took on many different names, and many different sectors of society from business to sports used the model, because every therapist wanted ownership of it in some way. Furthermore, psychologists used it in therapy to treat any condition related to lack of self-confidence, not just depression.

Thousands of people have used this life hack to reclaim, rebuild, and enrich their lives after years of depression, addiction, social anxiety disorders, self-esteem issues, and even schizophrenia. Pro athletes use it and so do successful businesspeople, law enforcement officers, doctors and dentists, lawyers, bankers and brokers, and others to improve their leadership abilities and overall performance, which also increases organizational effectiveness.

The principles of ACT are sometimes called Mindfulness-Acceptance-Commitment Approach, Mindfulness-Based

Emotional Intelligence Training, Psychological Flexibility Training, and Acceptance and Commitment Treatment.

Regardless of the name, it is successful in its innovative approach to developing mindfulness. Mindfulness is the state of being aware, open, and focused. Mindfulness allows us to be completely engaged in what we are doing in order to make sound decisions. Instead of permitting our emotions to make the decisions for us, we use our rational mind instead. The art of mindfulness evolved in Eastern philosophy thousands of years ago, and Western civilization has practiced aspects of it through ancient doctrines such as mediation, yoga, tai chi, martial arts, and ZEN.

However, with ACT, you do not have to follow any ancient tradition, and through its practice, you can develop mindfulness skills in a short amount of time. The three mindfulness skills that you must develop to increase your awareness through your trek to reduce your fear and anxiety, and increase your confidence are the following:

- **Defusion** is the first skill, which is not to be confused with "diffusion." Diffusion is the act of spreading of a tangible thing more widely. Defusion is a psychological term that deals with the separation of emotion-provoking stimulus from its unwanted emotional response. In other words, defusion also gives you the power to separate from your thoughts. Your thoughts come and then go without inciting pain, fear or self-defeating beliefs to dismantle your self-confidence.

- **Expansion** is the power to open up and make space for difficult emotions, feelings, and sensations like anger, fear, and anxiety, without allowing them to overpower your actions. Like defusion, the emotions come and go without ever pulling you into pieces or pushing you around.

- **Engagement** is the power to live in the moment and be aware of what is occurring to you RIGHT NOW, not yesterday and not tomorrow. This includes not allowing your thoughts to consume you as you curiously venture and actively immerse yourself completely into every moment.

Moreover, you must clarify your values in order to establish how you want to live as a person in the world. Those values, which we will discuss in a later section, provide the blueprint for your life's goals and inspire your dedication to mindfulness. When values and mindfulness come together along with committed action, which means mental and emotional exercises and practice, you learn to become self-confident.

Your Jagged Thoughts

Your thoughts work against you. If you lack confidence, it is because of a dialogue that goes on in your mind when you step outside of your comfort zone. This dialogue began a while ago. The internal conversation might go back so far that you do not even remember when it began.

It starts with something like this:

➢ You are going to screw this task up, for sure.

➢ This is bound to go wrong if you attempt this task.

> ➢ You are still not ready to take on this task.

> ➢ You are not good enough to do this task.

> ➢ You are going to embarrass yourself if you try this task.

> ➢ This task is too hard and you cannot do it.

What do you do to change the dialogue? You can challenge it by finding evidence to the contrary. You can replace them with positive thoughts. You can distract yourself from the thoughts. You might have heard these remedies before, and they might work temporarily, but we are looking for a permanent fix. If you have tried these ways of "deflection," you might have noticed that they burn up energy, your mind returns at some point to the negative internal conversation, and they might work in practice, but they dissolve when a real, high-level challenge presents itself.

You should not have to grit your teeth and go into what feels like a battle, and it is not very helpful to push the fear away or distract ourselves from it because fear is useful. There is logic to anxiety; in fact, being fearless is what is irrational. Negative thoughts are not the problem because our thoughts should not control our actions. Negative thoughts are not self-defeating or harmful.

The properties of ACT provide a different approach, and thank goodness for it. The solution is to not allow yourself to get caught up in the negative thoughts, and the term for responding to our thoughts is fusion. When you fuse things together, they become one, so you are looking to defuse the negative thoughts from your actions. You do not have to battle these thoughts; you subdue them to reduce their impact. The next sections explains how to do it.

Day 5:
Defusing Your Thoughts

"Focus means eliminating distractions, not just from other people, but the things we do to distract ourselves."

Catherine Pulsifer

There are two outcomes to allowing negative thoughts to invade our mind and take over our psyche. We quit our task or we continue through the task unfocused. Therefore, they must be "defused."

What does your mind say to you on a regular basis?

Is your mind kind to you? Is your mind truthful? Is your mind always pragmatic? Is your mind positive?

Normally, these are not the case if you lack self-confidence. When confidence is lacking, your mind only has good things to say when you decide to put off a task for a later time and provides you with momentary relief from an anxious exercise that will evolve you.

Before the good thoughts and feelings emerged when you made the decision to not practice, you were probably hit with something like, "I'm not in the mood," "It's too difficult," or "I'll do it some other time."

Despite your best intentions, your mind plays dirty tricks on you in order to take the easy route and sidestep challenges. You would think that your own mind would have your best interests, and it would not call you names when you challenge yourself or offer you relief when you quit or put important things off, but it does, all the time.

Our mind baits us in many ways, and here are some of the ways that might be familiar to you:

- **Your mind compares you to other people** in detrimental ways, saying that you are not as talented, you are not as smart, or you that life is not as easy for you.

- Your mind provides you with all of the ways you are not up to the task through **self-judgment**.

- Your mind provides you with **obstacles** by showing you all of the difficulties that are in front of you.

- **Your mind predicts failure**, rejection, and other unpleasant outcomes.

To see which set of excuses your mind provides, challenge it. In fact, challenge yourself today. Do something simple today that it outside of your comfort zone that will improve your life and would be a show of confidence. It must be something that you have never done before.

We are giving you permission to put down the book and exercise a show of self-confidence. Write down your goal, and do not read the next paragraph until you have completed the practice session.

Did you do take the challenge? Yes? Congratulations! What were the voices saying to you as you approached the challenging moment? What reasons did your mind provide to you in an attempt to try to talk you out of it?

Did you do the challenge? No? If you didn't follow through on the challenge, what reasons did your mind give you to skip the exercise?

It is important to know which of the four reasons your mind gave you. Did it self-judge you, provide obstacles, predict failure, or compare you in a negative way to other people? It is important to understand your trigger as you continue to read and evolve.

Day 6:
Know Your Personal Values

"When your values are clear to you, making decisions becomes easier."

Roy E. Disney

You cannot set goals for yourself unless you are keenly aware of your personal values. If you do not understand why you created your goals, you will lose focus as you travel the path or you will completely give up on your goals as you move through difficult times while seeking to obtain them.

Values inspire us to continue on when things get rough. They motivate us through difficult days, setbacks, and failures. Values provide us with direction and keep us on track. Stand for something meaningful in your life, and for your life, and you will find fulfillment and satisfaction as you reach for your goals, even on your most difficult days; and remember that disappointment is certain if you create goals that do not align with your core beliefs. You must also know that victory on a daily basis lies within yourself, and there is personal glory in being true to your ideals even when no one is watching, and even when no one else cares.

Clarify your values, set goals that are in harmony with them, and then break the goals down into actions. Once you have actions, engage fully in them in order to "act" with confidence, and the "actions" will become feelings in time.

First, define your values; we have provided a list of common ones that were inspired by the book *Curious?* by Todd

Kashdan, who is a professor of psychology at George Mason University. There are no "right" or "wrong" values, so you will find some values on the list to be of little importance to you, while other values are crucial to your core beliefs and provide the bedrock of your identity, even if they are not currently in practice because of a limited self-confidence.

Go through the list and write down those things that are the most important to you, which are also the things that you want to start doing, or want to start doing better. The best part about going through the list is that we will show you how to attain these valuable character assets.

1) **Be accepting** of yourself, other people, and life

2) Actively **seek adventure** and stimulating experiences

3) **Be assertive** when respectfully standing up for yourself or requesting your needs

4) **Be authentic** so that you are genuine and real in every situation, and true to yourself

5) Appreciate, create, or **cultivate beauty** in yourself, other people, and the world

6) **Be caring** toward yourself, others, and the world

7) **Be challenging of yourself** to grow, learn, and improve

8) **Be compassionat**e towards those who are suffering

9) **Be respectful and obedient of obligations** and standards

10) Connect and **engage fully** with others and activities

11) **Contribute** to make a positive difference to yourself and others

12) **Cooperate and collaborate** with others

13) **Be courageous** in the face of fear, difficulty, and threat

14) **Be creative or innovative**

15) **Be curious** to explore and discover

16) **Be encouraging** to reward behavior that you value in yourself or others

17) **Be equitable** in the way you view and treat others and yourself

18) **Seek excitement** and engage in stimulating activities

19) **Be fair** to yourself and others

20) **Be physically and mentally fit** to improve your well-being

21) **Be flexible** to adjust and adapt to every situation

22) **Be forgiving** towards yourself and others

23) **Live freely** and to help others do the same

24) **Be friendly** and agreeable towards others

25) **Seek fun**, and create and engage in enjoyable activities

26) **Be generous** to yourself and others

27) **Be grateful** and appreciate the positive things about yourself, others, and the world

28) **Be honest**, truthful, and sincere with yourself and others

29) **Be humble** and modest and let your achievements speak for themselves

30) **Find humor** and show it and appreciate it

31) **Be independent** to support yourself and choose your own way of doing things

32) **Be industrious**, hardworking, and dedicated

33) **Be open to intimacy** emotionally or physically in close personal relationships

34) **Uphold justice** and fairness

35) **Be kind**, compassionate, considerate, or nurturing towards yourself or others

36) **Act lovingly** or affectionately towards yourself or others

37) **Be mindful** and curious about my immediate experience

38) **Be open-minded** to weighing evidence objectively, see other points of view, and thinking things through

39) **Be orderly** and organized

40) **Be patient** and wait calmly with tolerance for what you want

41) **Be persistence** to continue resolutely despite the situation

42) **Seek pleasure** for yourself and give pleasure to others

43) **Be powerful** to influence, show authority, take charge, or lead

44) **Be reciprocative** to build relationships that are fair and balanced

45) **Be respectful** towards yourself and others, and be polite and considerate

46) **Be responsible** and accountable for your actions

47) **Be romantic** to display and express love or affection

48) **Be safe** to secure, protect, or ensure the safety of yourself or others

49) **Be self-aware** of your thoughts, feelings, and actions

50) **Be self-caring** to look after your health and well-being, and get your needs met

51) **Be self-developmental** to keep growing, advancing, or improving in knowledge, skills, character, or life experience

52) **Show self-control** to act in accordance with your ideals

53) **Be Sensual** to create, explore, and enjoy experiences that stimulate the five senses

54) **Be sexual** to explore or express your sexuality

55) **Be spirituality** to connect with things bigger than yourself

56) **Be skillful** to continually practice and improve your skills and apply yourself full

57) **Be supportive** to be helpful, encouraging, and available to yourself or others

58) **Be trustworthy** to be loyal, faithful, sincere, and able

59) Be (insert your own value if we missed yours)

All of these items require self-confidence to do them, so what you might find is that you have the confidence to do some things, but other things are more difficult for you, and the wall that keeps you from doing those things that you hold as valuable can shatter your self-confidence.

Now, pick out the five most important qualities that you want to accomplish each day. Are their gaps between the values you chose and your actions? If so, there is no reason to be upset. Grab a blank piece of paper and write down the five values that you chose as most important to you and read them aloud at the beginning of each day. Then, go into the day with a vision of accomplishing them.

Then, at the end of each day, read the values again and determine which ones you accomplished and which ones did not take form. Evaluate the reasons why you did not find your way to your core values, and figure out ways to improve the next day. Writing them down and saying them helps you draw inspiration and puts you in touch with them whenever you need them. You have to know where your core beliefs stand before you can ever grow self-confidence, but you must also remember that you should not calculate your self-worth based upon whether you met your values. You should see gradual growth with time and thoughtful management of your five items, but they are not rigid rules that determine whether you are a good or bad person.

You must hold onto your values lightly while pursuing them with vigor, and stand by the belief that success comes through living your life through your values, and nothing else. You obtain other things of worth by living a life based on your values, and people might define those things you achieve as "success," and that is fine. However, you must remember in your heart that the success came by completely living through you core beliefs and never separating yourself from them.

Day 7:
Practice

"Knowledge is of no value unless you put it into practice."

Anton Chekhov

Before we get too far, we need to address an issue that is very common among those of us who tend to lack confidence; we do not like exercises that force us to practice elements of self-confidence. One thing is clear, you are reading this book because you understand that increasing your self-confidence will increase your fulfillment in life. Yet, taking the hard steps to get there might sound painful. The most painful part of the process to becoming self-confident is the PRACTICE part of it.

There is a lot of practice to come.

Practice is required to get good at anything; therefore, it is no different when it comes to self-confidence. Practice does not sound terrible until you find out what it entails, which is stepping WAY outside your comfort zone, and stepping into the briar patch and its menacing thorns is uncomfortable and creates anxiety. In fact, deciding NOT to practice feels like a better idea, and the relief at making the decision to avoid exercises to increase our confidence, feels like something close to an accomplishment, because it feels so darn good, but we know very well that it is not an achievement. By not practicing, the habit of "avoidance" forms, becoming second nature, and long-term fulfillment is lost over temporary comfort.

Psychologists call the choice to forgo practice "experiential avoidance." This fancy term means that you choose to avoid any thoughts, feelings, physical sensations, and memories that cause discomfort, though it maintains ongoing psychological distress. In order to defeat this phenomenon, you have to open ourselves up to the experiences that make us uncomfortable in order to relieve the internal pain. In other words, you are required to practice through performance exercises, so that you participate in life-enhancing things.

You might choose to call the exercises "unimportant" in order to make yourself feel better. You might say that you will do the exercise later when you have the time. We know better; you will not make the time unless the time is now, and that is why we are here. You are attempting to be true to yourself, to become a confident person, and to make choices that benefit you long term, and your practice sessions must begin today. If you chose to bypass the exercises in the past sections, you must do them today, and continue doing them until you catch up because the excuses stop and the confidence starts today.

What gets you through the discomfort, anxiety, fatigue, frustration, and fear?

Your core values get you there.

They work better than any motivational poster or quote. They have more strength than positive thinking exercises and self-affirmations.

Day 8:
The "New" Failure

"I've missed more than 9,000 shots in my career. I've lost almost three hundred games. Twenty-six times I've been trusted to take the game-winning shot...and missed. I've failed over and over and over again in my life. That is why I succeed."

Michael Jordan

While learning to do anything better, we are going make many mistakes on the journey. In fact, the further we adventure into new territory, the more blunders we will make. No one likes making mistakes, but failure is an essential part of our self-development throughout life, and fighting it is futile. It is best to accept it, as every successful person has done.

When a reporter asked the president of IBM, Thomas Watson, to provide his formula for success, he responded, "Double your rate of failure." Watson understands that risk-taking, making mistakes, and failing was the equation for achievement on any level. American philosopher John Dewey went further to say, "Failure is instructive. The person who really thinks, learns quite as much from his failures as from his successes."

While it is easy to rationalize the notion that failure is a part of any great accomplishment, it is more difficult to embrace because failure never feels good. There is a divide between our current situation, which lacks self-confidence, and a new reality. Closing that gap is a painful process, and the wider the divide, the more pain you must endure, if you find failure painful. While we walk the tightrope from lack of confidence to self-assurance, failure pulls away the rope, and we fall often.

No one likes to feel uncomfortable feelings, so to avoid painful situations, we often quit, or worse, we give up before we even get started. Instead, we take the easy route and avoid the challenges that might hurt us. Quitting provides relief, but never lasts. In the end, it never feels good to quit, and when we reside inside our comfort zone for too long, there is a heavy feeling of loss that accompanies it. There is always calm in stagnant waters, but standing water that does not flow is stale and foul. Before long, we are beating ourselves up for continuing down the same road that gets us nowhere fast.

People fail:

- Albert Einstein failed. He wanted to attend the prestigious Swiss Polytechnic Institute, but he failed the entrance exam.

- Oprah Winfrey failed. She was told that she "wasn't fit for television" when she lost her job as a news anchor in Baltimore.

- Walt Disney failed. His first animation studio lasted just one month before it went broke.

- Steven Spielberg failed. He applied three times to the University of Southern California School of Theater, Film, and Television, but the college did not accept him.

- Bill Gates and Paul Allen failed. Their first business, which measured traffic flow, never met its mark, and

Gates now says, "When the guy from the County came to see it, it didn't work."

- Abraham Lincoln failed, a lot. America's greatest president was defeated in his run for Illinois House of Representatives. When he lost, he opened a store, which went bankrupt within months.

These famous and innovate people revel in their stories of failure because it shows their fortitude. When you fail, you certainly are in good company.

When I fail, and my mind slips a bit, to where I am unable to defuse my emotions from my actions for a moment, I end it all by allowing myself permission to make mistakes, and even to be STUPID. I will not allow the tyranny of the dictator inside my head who calls me stupid, and I remind myself that if I keep pushing, the only option the universe will allow is that I get better at the task I am attempting to accomplish.

There is no more honest feedback than failure; the best of us receive poor reviews at times, and we rebound from our negative critique with the productive criticism in hand to fight another day. Thomas Edison did not allow his lack of success to halt his momentum to inventing the light bulb. To the contrary, he did not even look at his endless unsuccessful experiments as failures. He famously said, "I haven't failed; I've just found ten thousand ways that won't work."

Remember that failure is a natural part of the learning process, and it allows us the opportunity to reflect on the things that did not work, and to rework our strategy to figure out what could potentially work better the next time around.

As Henry Ford put it, "Failure provides the opportunity to begin again, more intelligently."

Furthermore, always remember that true success is living by your values, and as we have discussed, if you always act on your values, then even if you do not readily achieve your goals, you are still a success. For example, if you were a writer who lived by the values of creativity, self-expression, and personal growth, would you consider yourself a failure if you wrote a book that could not find a publisher? We hope not. Alternatively, say that a publisher printed your book, but it got bad reviews. Does this make you a failure? No, it does not if you look at the experience from a values-focused perspective. Both of the outcomes are irrelevant. The important thing would be that you lived the experience through your values and found the PROCESS rewarding, challenging, and fulfilling.

This notion needs to be your NEW failure, but how do you rebound from those experiences that sure did feel like failure and are holding you back from new experiences and self-confidence? The next section provides valuable steps to get you back on track.

Day 9:
Rebound from Perceived Failure

Success is the ability to go from failure to failure without loss of enthusiasm"

Winston Churchill

Are you perfect yet?

If you beat yourself up after every mistake, and you punish yourself by hiding from tasks that remind you of your failure, it must have worked, right?

No, these things are horrible ways to approach your mistakes, and they get you nowhere. When you fail, it should provide encouragement to continue instead of incentive to punish yourself.

When you want to get your horse to move, do you beat it with a stick or do you dangle a carrot in front of its face and give it the carrot once you reach your destination? Both work, but a horse that is beaten will be unhealthy and unhappy, and hold an endless grudge against you. The carrot is the better option, and you should find your carrot instead of railing against yourself when you make mistakes, or worse, blaming other people for your failures.

There are five steps to rebound from a failure, and you should look to them whenever a mistake knocks you off your feet and abruptly stops your momentum:

1. **Notice your name-calling and neutralize it**. While you are busy calling yourself an "Idiot!" or "Loser!" or "Quitter!" recognize the whipping you are delivering to yourself. Say, "there is the idiot-loser-quitter story again; the one I am so good at delivering." Then, thank your mind for its criticism, let the thoughts go, and immediately begin focusing on your task again.

2. **Observe the painful sensations within yourself**, breathe deeply, and open up some space around them. In addition, and this might sound crazy, but it works: if you are somewhere in privacy, place your hand where it hurts the most, and gently hold the pain. Even tough guys who find the act effeminate find the process useful once they got past their reluctance.

3. **Be good to yourself**. It is unhealthy for your esteem to belittle yourself endlessly after every mistake you mistake. It is equally unhealthy to tell yourself to "suck it up" and be strong. That kind of attitude is not true mental toughness, which is the ability to continue on your task even when it hurts. In order to develop real mental fortitude, self-acceptance, self-kindness, and a commitment to core values are required. Think of it this way. How would you comfort someone you love after they have failed? Do you beat them down and call them a loser? No, you do not treat them cruelly. Learn to love yourself, and when mistakes happen, talk to yourself in a compassionate way. However, you must find middle ground. On one hand, do not point the finger and judge yourself, do not call yourself a coward for the fear inside of you, but also, do not sugarcoat the situation or try to fix things with internal dialogue. Trying to fix the

situation through positive affirmation might seem like the right thing to do, but it leads to frustration, irritation, and disappointment when words alone do not get you back on task. In these moments of rebound, you need self-empathy and genuine good will towards yourself. Instead of clichés like "every cloud has a silver lining" and "Rome wasn't built in a day," try something sincere in your internal dialogue. Consider the following dialogue: "This is understandably painful, and we can take some time to absorb the hurt, but let's keep on pushing onward to attain our goals because there is value in them, and we will become a better person through the process and find more rewards at the end."

4. You did something right, so **appreciate even the smallest thing that worked**. These things provide a foundation for building. First, you stepped into the fire and that is a big deal. Second, you have critical information to draw upon now that you can only gather by doing. And guess what? The world did not crumble around you and you survived. Third, whether it was a small detail that worked for you or something that worked very well, you improved. You showed courage and self-confidence, no matter how big or small, and you should reward yourself because of it. Ineffective self-coaching involves only focusing on the things that went wrong. Acknowledge and appreciate what you did right, spend some time considering what went wrong, and rework the process in order to get the most use out of the time you spent becoming a better person and growing as an individual.

5. **Stand up for yourself**. You enhanced your life and you did not give up. Never mind the critics, especially the ones in your head, and remember that you persisted, you learned, you showed courage, you adapted, and you grew. Think about the future for a minute as you marinate in your mistakes (accomplishment); you will one day look back with pride at how you reached for more out of life through trying times. One day, you will laugh at your stumbles, and share your gaffes with people who lack self-confidence and look to you for inspiration. You will have it all one day as long as you hold onto your values and carry on.

In his book *Touching the Void*, Joe Simpson recounts his nearly fatal descent off a mountain in the Peruvian Andes. During a fall down an ice cliff, he crushed his tibia, breaking his right leg. With no drinking water or food and bad weather pressing upon him, he came out alive. In the midst of despair and hopelessness, he heard encouraging words from inside himself that pulled him through. "The voice" reminded him of the things he needed to do to survive, and not the trouble all around him.

Failure sure does hurt sometimes, but there is no better teacher.

Day 10:
Motivation is a Trap

"The problem with making an extrinsic reward the only destination that matters is that some people will choose the quickest route there, even if it means taking the low road. Indeed, most of the scandals and misbehavior that have seemed endemic to modern life involve shortcuts."

Daniel H. Pink

You are motivated. Your every action requires motivation because the intention of every action is to achieve something, and that achievement is called motivation. There is a purpose behind everything you do, whether you are reading this book, eating a bagel, driving your car, crafting a speech, searching for buried treasure, or delaying self-confidence practice. We may not be consciously aware of every motivation, but even if we are not conscious of every motivating factor that influences our decisions, we are in the middle of several tasks that motivation propels at all times, until we die.

Motivation is not magic and it does not have any real power. It is a "thing" that simply provides us with the desire to do something. Furthermore, motivation is NOT a feeling. If we relied on the "right feeling" to provide us with the motivation to do any action, we would get nowhere fast. Motivation is desire, and we often have competing desires. One desire tells us to remain in our comfort zone because it supplies momentary relief, and if you have been paying attention, you know the other desire is to act on our values.

These two warring motivations will pull you down two very different paths when you hit a fork in the road. One path is an avoidance-driven life that has few rewards and the other is a value-driven life that has endless bounty. The way we shift from the human instinct to find immediate comfort to values and long-term satisfaction is to emphasize the ideals of "commitment" over motivation.

Having desire does not equate to being committed. Many of us wait until the day we feel confident to take action. Many of us wait our entire lives. During certain tasks, your stomach might be in knots, your heart might race, and your mind might attempt to convince you that it is not worth the tension you feel. Quitting becomes an incredibly irresistible idea. You have to force yourself into action because of a commitment to values. The actions of confidence come before the feelings of confidence, and commitment comes before motivation. In time, you will feel inspired, joyful, and energized when your self-confidence builds and you are a bigger part of the world.

Part Two:
Engage in Life

Day 11:
Engagement is Powerful

"The more you engage and connect, the more engagements and connections you will have."

Loren Weisman

If you want to get the most fulfillment from life and develop a sense of confidence, you have to be aware, attentive, and engaged in all of your experiences. This involves the basic building block of mindfulness called "engagement."

During "engagement," you connect to the world through the use of all of your senses. You notice every nuance as you go about an activity or task. This requires that you defuse your thoughts; therefore, every self-judgment or negative thought that enters your brain is pushed away, so that you stay in the moment.

With anything that you do, you have to be psychologically present to be good at it. In other words, you need to be engaged in what is happening. Take sex, for example. Some people have so many hang-ups about sex that they perform poorly or cannot perform at all. Instead of experiencing an intimate moment with a spouse or partner, some individuals are thinking about numerous things that have nothing to do with the person in front of them and the action at hand. They think, "I wonder how he or she thinks that I am doing," or "I wonder what he or she thinks of my body," or "I wonder if I will be able to perform at all."

The thoughts of anyone engaged in a healthy round of sex should be on all of the pleasurable sensations that accompany it, including the touch and feel of naked skin, the warmth and friction of two bodies in motion, and the breathing and vocalizations of the partner. All other thoughts should float on by, pushed away by the beautiful moment in front of you.

This is true of any situation both professional and friendly. You become better at everything that has your full attention and your commitment to engaging in it.

Imagine you are in an interview, and instead of focusing on the interviewer and engaging in the questions, negative thoughts and self-judgments consume you. While the interviewer is asking questions, you think, "I am unqualified," "I will fail," I am so boring," or "I have never done a good interview in my life."

How do you think you will fair? Will you get the job? No, you get the job if you are engaged in the task, not bad past experiences, not self-defeating thoughts, and not criticisms of your approach.

When we say that someone looks confident, it is because we can see how he or she is behaving and we can observe what he or she is doing. We have no way of telling what they are thinking. We have no idea how they are feeling. What we notice most about confident people is they are VERY ENGAGED in what they are doing. When they socialize, they are thoroughly in the moment of the conversation. When they give a presentation, they are completely focused on the task. Next time you see a confident person consider these things.

When we keep our attention on what we are doing and remain fully engaged in the task, then it does not matter what our minds tell us. Our thoughts create problems if they bait us into drifting into their stream instead of allowing them to pass. If you let them come, and let them go, then your attention remains on important issues.

Day 12:
"Being in the Moment"

"The secret of health for both mind and body is not to mourn for the past, worry about the future, or anticipate troubles, but to live in the present moment wisely and earnestly."

Buddha

We will only feel confident when we are able to do something well. However, it is impossible to do anything well if we are not engaged in what we are doing. If we just go about our tasks mindlessly, while lost in our own thoughts, or we go through our life on autopilot, we will never perform anything well.

Therefore, it is crucial that we fully engage in all of our activities, and I will say something that I do not say a lot in this book. It is SIMPLE to engage. We pay attention and notice what is occurring around us. While mindfulness requires a lot of practice and is difficult at every step, paying attention is not, and paying attention is the core of mindfulness.

So, it starts with paying attention, but to get to the next level, we must pay attention in a brand new way, which will bring us close to mindfulness. Mindfulness means that we pay attention to the world around us and every task with curiosity, flexibility, and openness.

Let us define each of them, so there is clarity on what you are attempting to do:

- **We pay attention** to what is happening in the moment, both in the physical world and what is going on inside of us. We notice what we are feeling and thinking, and how the physical world is influencing our senses. We register everything that we see, hear, touch, taste, and smell.

- **We are curious** about the things that are happening around us. Furthermore, we actively seek to discover something brand new in our experience that we may have missed in the past or taken for granted. You become an adventurer everyday and explore the world in a brand new way to find the intricate detail in everything.

- **We are open** to everything that is happening, even those things that we do not align with, including spiritually and politics. We do not turn away from any experience, or shut off our mind simply because we disagree with it or disapprove of it. Learn about all things that come your way because it is important to your growth and confidence as a person and scientist learning the world again.

- **We are flexible** in the ways in which we pay attention. We adapt to our surroundings. We may have a laser focus when we need it. That narrow look at things is required when we are cutting vegetables, hammering a nail, or hitting a golf ball. However, much of the time, we have broad focus when we are hiking through the woods or exploring a carnival. In these situations, we take in all of the smells, sounds, and sights. Moreover, we may move back and forth between what we are feeling inside of us and what are experiencing in the physical world.

Try it right now. Stop reading for a moment and pay attention to the world around you. Notice your current feelings from the sounds that are coming from you that include your movements and breathing, and the sounds all around you, which could be anything from the tick of a clock, the hum of a refrigerator, to a plane overhead. Maybe you are in a more magical place such as the beach, and I hope that is the case; truly experience all of its power. What do you see wherever you might be? Notice color, shape, texture, shadows and highlights, as if you are a photographer or an artist who is telling a visual story and does not want to miss a thing. What do you feel on your skin? What do you smell?

While you were reading, you had a narrow focus, but when you escaped from the words for a minute, your focus broadened. You became "present" when you saw the design in everything. We all spend a lot of time lost in negative thoughts in the screens of a phone, tablet, or television, and we lose our sense of self, and our place in the world when we do. Self-confidence is lost when we do not appreciate our little space in the greater scheme of things. We are a piece of the puzzle, and it is a very important piece, that gets lost when we are not present to enjoy the wonders in the world.

Most importantly for those who lack self-confidence, we have a tendency to get lost in the words inside our head, instead of paying attention to all aspects of our experience. When you learn to engage and be mindful, the thoughts that control your fears begin to disappear.

Day 13:
Mindfulness

"People usually consider walking on water or in thin air a miracle. But I think the real miracle is not to walk either on water or in thin air, but to walk on earth. Every day we are engaged in a miracle, which we don't even recognize: a blue sky, white clouds, green leaves, and the black, curious eyes of a child—our own two eyes. All is a miracle."

Thich Nhat Hanh

If a thought is helpful, it contains useful information that helps us perform better. When the information is helpful, we can use the information to take positive actions. Unhelpful thoughts must be let go. If we could avoid the negative thoughts altogether, it would be wonderful, but even Zen masters cannot control every negative notion after years of practice, so you would be wasting your time to try. Instead, learn mindfulness skills.

Mindfulness is a hard skill to learn, so practice is required. With the help of a few exercises, your mindfulness will progressively build. There must be easier ways to learn to be mindful, right? No, there is no easy approach. You do not get on a bike and ride it perfectly on your first attempt. It takes some courage, numerous falls, many scrapes, and some wobbling even when you develop the knack for doing it.

> Do you give up then?

> Do you read a book on how to ride a bike?

No, you get on the bike and practice. I wish you could go back in time and enjoy the smile on your face and the joy in your heart when you grasped the skill of riding a bike for the first time, as you sailed away down the street like a pro.

That can happen with mindfulness. That can happen once you use mindfulness to improve your self-confidence.

Life is a show like no other. On life's stage, we have memories through images, and physical and mental sensations in all the things that we see, hear, touch, taste, and smell, and through our thoughts and memories. In that show called life, mindfulness is the lighting that is so crucial to the production of any stage performance. Without the lighting, we lose the details of the show. Sometimes, the lighting is broad to capture all of the action or the light is only a beam to spotlight something important.

For your show, focus on whatever is the most important thing in every moment. Pay attention to the things that help you be the person we want to become, and do things that you WANT TO DO. Psychologists call this "task-focused attention," which means that you are completely focused on the task in front of you.

If you want to perform a task well, you center your full attention on whatever is important and relevant to the task in front of you. Negative self-judgments and predictions that you will fail or you are simply not good enough are irrelevant parts of your show. However, it is difficult to get them off your stage because they do not just disappear into an abyss. Everyone encounters their fears, but you can figure out ways to place a spotlight on the important parts of your task and dim the lights on the self-judgments. There is an exercise called mindful breathing that can help you immensely.

Mindful breathing is a practice that is thousands of years old. We find it in the diverse spiritual and philosophical traditions of Buddhism, Hinduism, Christianity, Judaism, Taoism, Islam, tai chi, yoga, and martial arts. It is simple and effective at developing engagement and defusion skills. You can do it for as long as necessary to get you through the negativity that clouds your mind and pulls you off task. Some do it for 30 seconds and some do it for 30 minutes. If this is your first go-around with mindful breathing, start with three minutes, and increase the duration, as you get better. The exercise might seem strange at first. You might be uncomfortable with its rhythms of focused deep breathing after years of unconscious shallow breathing. You might get light-headed or feel anxious as you practice, but if you stick with the breathing, it will make more sense and feel natural within a week.

Here are the steps to how it works:

1) Get into a comfortable position. A good position is one in which you are seated upright in a chair with your back straight and your feet flat on the ground.

2) You can close your eyes or focus your gaze on particular spot.

3) Take gentle, slow breaths through your nostrils with a focus on emptying your lungs. Calmly push out all of the air from your lungs and then allow your lungs to fill back up themselves. In other words, you do not have to fill them back up; they automatically refill.

4) You are an explorer who is observing your breathing pattern for the first time. Notice all sensations, which include the air moving into your nose, and the air moving out of it. Notice the rise and fall of your shoulders, your chest, yours ribs, and your abdomen. Notice the effortless way that all of this occurs with the simple passing of air into your lungs.

5) Take ten breaths with a natural rhythm that places a spotlight on your breath. Let your thoughts glide away like a plane across the sky. Many things will pass through your mind as you breathe, from dinner plans, to old memories, to your busy day ahead or behind you. When these thing grab hold of you, acknowledge their appearance and gently push them away.

6) You might beat yourself up because you do not think you are doing the exercise well, and you might get bored or frustrated, so name the feelings and then refocus on your breathing. With each acknowledgment and reengagement with your breathing, you are developing a skill that will improve the most important aspect of building up your self-confidence, and that is sustained focus.

7) When you have completed the exercise, expand your awareness and engage with the world again. However, maintain your spotlight on your breathing as you slowly remove the spotlight and turn on the lights to your physical body and the environment around you. Push your feet solidly into the floor, sit up straight, stretch, and notice everything through all of your senses. What can you see, hear, smell, touch, and taste?

8) You exercise is complete.

Give it a shot. Stop reading, find a spot, and practice for the first time. Create a schedule for formal practice. Set aside three minutes for two or three days each day to sit quietly and practice your breathing. Then, increase the duration by 30 seconds each week, until you get to ten minutes for two or three times a day.

Day 14:
Ways to Practice Mindfulness

"If you want to conquer the anxiety of life, live in the moment, live in the breath."

Amit Ray

We can focus on many things for long periods of time. We can sit in a movie theater and be completely engrossed in a good movie for two hours. We can sit in a hammock and read a book for an hour without distraction. We can play a game of chess or basketball without ever losing focus. We engage in conversations the keep our attention for 15-30 minutes, or more. All of these things are "within" our comfort zone, but when we step out of comforting situations to engage in a new task, it becomes a real challenge to maintain our focus.

Mindful breathing is a super way to practice and improve your focus skills. You can enhance the eight steps to make the breathing exercise more interesting or easier.

Consider the following:

- Silently count every breath you take, saying the number as you exhale. When you reach ten, go back to one and begin again.

- Repeat the actions through words as you breathe in and out. For example, "in," and "out," or "focus in," and "focus out."

- Visualize your breath as a color that is flowing into and out of your lungs.

- Visualize your breath as a white cloud heading into your nostrils and a black cloud as it leaves your body.

- Visualize your lungs as balloons that expand and contract with each breath.

There are many places that you can practice your breathing exercises:

- Waiting in line

- On a plane

- Waiting at a traffic light (stare into the red light)

- On the commode

- During a commercial

- During the trailers at the theater

- In bed

- While you are on hold

- Any stressful moment when you are anxiously waiting for something to occur

Mindful breathing is a great start to improving your self-confidence. In the middle of your busy daily routines, you can create a restful state that recharges your batteries and offers you some inner peace. However, it is also a training mechanism to teach you how to engage. Thereby, when you are performing a meaningful task, such as giving a speech, negotiating that deal, or playing a competitive game of golf, you shine your mindfulness spotlight on the activity instead of breathing. Engage fully in the task as you allow your negative thoughts that include self-judgment to pass like a log in a stream.

What else can you do to find your focus? The next section will guide you.

Day 15:
Engage in All Things

"Be happy in the moment, that's enough. Each moment is all we need, not more."

Mother Teresa

In his autobiography, *Long Walk to Freedom*, revolutionary Nelson Mandela described his 20-minute march from his demoralizing prison cell to a rock quarry as a "tonic." At the quarry, Mandela and other prisoners toiled away with bleeding and blistered hands as they picked and shoveled rocks all day under a scorching South African sun on Robben Island. Mandela, who led the movement to end apartheid in South Africa, cracked rocks for thirteen years.

He engaged in every moment of the experience that crumbled weaker men. He watched the birds, he felt the wind off the sea, he smelt blossoming eucalyptus, and he felt his pounding muscles and battered hands. He did not think about the hours that he had left in the grinding day, the situation that put him in prison, or the dreadful years of prison live that were ahead.

Under the worst conditions, Mandela was mindful, and not on autopilot. He engaged in the moment and it got him through. You can do the same under less miserable conditions. You can connect with all of your senses in order to find fulfillment in everyday as you build your self-confidence.

Do you ever stop to smell the rose? Do you ever ponder your fortune that you can stop and engage in a moment, instead of locking yourself into self-judging thoughts, painful past outcomes, and negative emotions?

I hope that you tried mindful breathing. I hope that you push through a month of it because you will find extraordinary results. If you do not, or you want to supplement it with other ways to find focus and engage your senses, there are other exercises at your disposal.

Remember, developing your ability to be present, focused, and fully engaged in everything you do is essential to do it well, and that is why we are still here and focusing on mindfulness. It is the key first and last step to being a better version of yourself.

You are probably busy. You might even tell yourself that you are too busy to complete exercises to get better and become more confident. However, there is no easy way around the path that takes you to a more blissful life. We do want to make the task to get there as easy as possible for you, so we have put together some more ways that you can practice during the course of the day that incorporate "the day" itself. Here are some options:

- **Turn your daily routines into practice sessions**. Engage in brushing your teeth, showering, shaving your face (guys) or legs (ladies), making your bed, preparing and eating your breakfast, driving your route to work, taking an elevator or walking stairs. Instead of moving through these activities on autopilot, engage in the plot of every activity using all five senses, almost as if you are doing them all for the first time. Recognize the smell of your soap, the gurgling of your coffee pot, the splash of milk into your bowl, the feeling of your razor or a vibrating shaver, and the taste of your toast. Notice your movements and the effortless way you move through every routine. Notice everything. Furthermore, when your thoughts turn to any stress about the busy day ahead, recognize the stress, and watch it pass through the air, and reengage in your task.

- **Turn your tedious chores into practice sessions**. Normally, you rush through your chores, whether you are bagging the leaves in your yard, loading the dishwasher, or folding clothes, you "do not" try to think about the chore or engage in it mindfully because you never saw any purpose in doing so. Well, there is purpose now. All of your chores proved a perfect time to engage in the moment. These provide is a great way to find the focus you need. Have you ever seen the move *The Truman Show* or the show *Big Brother*? The first is a fiction movie about a person whose life is broadcast live every moment of the day, and the second is a reality show that does the same. So, think of yourself with cameras on you and millions of people watching you as you stack wood, mop the floor, or mow your yard. How do you want to present your chore to the world? Or, you can imagine that you are giving a class on changing your car oil or raking leaves. Every step is done deliberately and with grace to show the world or your class how good you are at performing your chore.

- **Turn your leisurely activities into practice sessions**. The first two examples are nothing that you could ever construe as fun, but they are important to your evolution. However, your leisurely or pleasurable activities can be done in the same way. Even the joyful tasks in our lives are ones that we normally take for granted. Stop doing that. Engage in them. From a walk through the park or woods, reading a story to your child, or eating a fantastic meal at your favorite restaurant. All of these things are enjoyable, but when we engage in them, we gain a new level of appreciation, and it is less likely that our minds wander from our good time to our work or other stresses. Hear the birds, feel the wind, small the air, enjoy the closeness with a child and an unfolding story, and taste, really taste, every morsel that you put into your mouth.

There are numerous, simple ways for you to develop mindfulness regardless of your busy life and impossible schedule. You can put your spotlight on anything at any time to exercise your engagement skills. The more you practice, the less likely you are to find yourself in a fog of discontent and lack of confidence.

Day 16:
"Self-Esteem" is a Myth

"Worry does not empty tomorrow of its sorrow, it empties today of its strength. If you want to be happy, do not dwell in the past, do not worry about the future, focus on living fully in the present. Instead of worrying about what you cannot control, shift your energy to what you can create."

Corrie ten Boom

Isn't it amazing that one major setback can shatter the confidence of highly successful people? A person could have a 20-year winning streak and a major setback sends him or her down a road towards hopelessness with a defeated soul and a miserable outlook on life. The self-esteem myth caught this person in its trap.

Humans divide people into two major categories: the winners and the losers. We are pushed to look at EVERYTHING as a win or a loss. You are a success or a failure, or you are a champ or a chump, and there is hardly any middle ground. Apparently, some formula that the world's citizens have put together tells us whether we have succeeded. A person comes in fourth place in the Olympics and is a failure, while the person who holds the gold medal receives glory.

Well, I am here to tell you that they both are winners. There is even a chance that the fourth-place finisher has had to work harder to overcome more obstacles than the gold-medal holder. However, society pigeonholes the "loser" immediately. We think, "They didn't want it as much," or they did not have the same amount of "willpower," "motivation," or "discipline" as the top three finishers did.

If you embrace the idea that you are a success or a "winner at life," there are only short-term benefits. Eventually, we look down the road to someone that we perceive as more successful. The comparison might bring about self-doubt, and before we know it, we lock ourselves into a battle with someone who could care less about us. They become our obsession, and instead of following values, we begin to head down a shadier path that eventually makes us feel dirty and unhappy.

People who go around with the mindset that they are "winners" usually have a fragile self-esteem. It is a very common trait among "successful" athletes, celebrities, and business professionals. Their lives are a series of "wins and losses," and if too many losses stack up or their performance drops, they immediately begin to wonder if they are a "loser," and once that gets into the heads of people who have always declared themselves successful, they bottom out. In between, there is constant desperation and fear because they tie everything into their status.

They cannot see the humor in anything, they take themselves too seriously, they begin to believe their own hype, and the fear of failure becomes their only fuel. Trailing them through their entire existence is chronic stress, burnout, and performance anxiety.

Weaknesses are a fundamental part of being human. Some of our "weaknesses" are fundamental to solid values. Forget the negative impact that chasing success has on our physical health, what about our soul? Winning leads to greed, cheating, and exploitation, all the way to a complete erosion of moral integrity and ethics.

All of these things rely upon self-esteem.

There is a cottage industry based upon it, and a world of people toss it about in their homes, classrooms, and playing fields. Self-esteem has quite the reputation these days as being a crucial part of the confidence we find in everything we do. If you have high self-esteem, you can certainly take over the world if you please, because you have it in you to do it.

Essentially, having a high self-esteem means that you evaluate yourself in a positive way. Keeping this definition in mind, consider the following notions:

- If you improve your self-esteem, you will improve your performance.

- If you improve your self-esteem, you will become more likable, have better social and professional relationships, and you will make a better impression on other people.

- If you improve your self-esteem, you will become a better leader.

Are these things true in your estimation?

In 2003 (or, what we like to refer to as a long time ago), the American Psychological Association investigated the claims that we made above. The Association commissioned a team of university psychologists to study decades of research on self-esteem to see if they could locate any evidence to confirm these popular ideas. You can find their results in a journal called *Psychological Science in the Public Interest*, but it does not appear that any parent, teacher, or life coach has ever read the findings. They certainly have not made the rounds and become public fodder that shatters long-established, self-esteem myths. If they were a part of the public forum, then we would know all of the following:

- High self-esteem does not improve performance, liability, relationships, or make people better leaders

- High self-esteem correlates with arrogance, narcissism, and egotism.

- High self-esteem correlates with prejudice and discrimination

- High self-esteem correlates with self-deception and defensiveness when faced with honest feedback

Ouch.

In fact, another study shows that people with low self-esteem who attempt to improve it through self-affirmation end up feeling worse.

So, what do you do instead? We will tell you in the next section.

Day 17:
Self-Acceptance

"Once we believe in ourselves, we can risk curiosity, wonder, spontaneous delight, or any experience that reveals the human spirit."

E.E. Cummings

Self-acceptance is far more important than self-esteem. When you head outside of your comfort zone, things will not always turn out the way you hope. Often, you will make mistakes, you will mess things up, and sometimes while cruising along at high speed without a worry in the world, you will hit speed bumps when you least expect them.

However, you will also achieve your goals.

When you fall, self-judgment should not lower upon you. Instead, self-acceptance should pick you up. Self-acceptance does not mean that you are not aware of the impact of your actions because it should never condone bad behavior. It simply means that you do not judge yourself for the mistakes you made while pursuing your goals through your values.

Judging yourself does not help you cause in any way. It does not enrich your life or make your life fuller. Knowing this from an intellectual perspective will not stop it from happening. We started judging ourselves in early childhood, so the pattern will not suddenly stop. However, you can unlatch yourself from our self-judgments, and you should begin the process now.

Practice unhooking your being from every form of self-judgment, and that includes the positive ones. You do not want to be stuck on any form of judgment. Imagine that your mind is a stream. Now, imagine the self-judgment as a log in the stream. There it goes. We see it float by; we see it float away. If your mind tells you that you are incompetent, notice it, name it as "negative judgment," and watch it float through your mind and away from you. If your mind is telling you that you are wonderful, notice it and name it: "positive judgment," and watch it sail away. You can even find humor as you watch them float by you. "Thank you so much for thinking that I am a wonderful person. Have a good day," or "That was not a very nice thing to say. Now, move along."

The story about you is not really you. Whether your mind describes you in wonderful ways or with hurtful criticism, they were only words and nothing more. Whether the words are true or false is irrelevant. What we really need to know is whether they are helpful. Do the words make our lives better? No, besides, they change all of the time and are unpredictable houseguests that rush into our minds without warning. For example, you leave the house in a great mood because you exercised and ate a healthy breakfast. You tell yourself that you did a great job and you are awesome. Then, you get in traffic, you get to work late to find a stack of work, and all of the good washes away because you start your day behind, and you tell yourself you are an idiot for not leaving your house earlier.

The trick is not to attach yourself to either one of the stories. Whether your mind says, "I'm awesome" or "I'm an idiot," "I'm a winner" or "I'm a loser," it is just a story. What matters the most are the things that you do, the way you behave, and the values that guide you. These things have far more value than the stories you tell about yourself during the day.

There is a huge difference between taking one's work seriously and taking one's self seriously. The first is crucial and the second will lead you to disaster.

If someone were presenting "you" right before you were going to give a presentation, would you want the person to say that they admire your values or that they admire your high opinion of yourself? Think about it in those terms. How do you want people to see you? Do you want people to think of you as a value-driven person or as a self-judgmental person?

Your life will become easier once you recognize that there are no losers, winners, failures or successes. We are humans who quit, who lose, and who fail. We are humans who follow through, win, and succeed. Every single one of us wins and loses, but it does not define us. A sure way to undermine your self-confidence is to dwell on your failures or your successes. If self-judgments are a pattern in your life, learn to notice them, name them, and neutralize them.

Part Three:
Inside the Confidence Game

Day 18:
Willpower and Discipline

"Try not to become a man of success, but rather a man of value."

Albert Einstein

You are probably thinking that I am going to try to sell you on the concepts of "willpower" and "discipline." Nope, to the contrary.

We have discussed "motivation," but two very close cousins are willpower and discipline, and you might catch yourself saying, "I am not disciplined," or "I have no willpower." Our minds latch onto these ideas and what start as only notions become a prophecy of things to come. They are fiction stories that you give the power to come true.

You might hold onto willpower and discipline as being tangible things that we must search for and find before we can begin living through our values and finding self-confidence along the way.

It only makes sense that you focus on these concepts because the world's gurus constantly tell us that we must possess the all-powerful discipline to do everything from learning to be patient with our spouse and children to walking two miles in the morning. Somehow, patience and exercise also require willpower. Unfortunately, if we put stock into these two things, we encounter an issue or two.

The first issue is that we put aside the important tasks like working on our self-confidence in order to run off looking for ways to have willpower and discipline. Once you read those books and take those course, you will find out you are missing something else. Then, a decade escapes you and you are still spinning your wheels. The second issue is that if you decided you just do not have the discipline and willpower to do what it takes to improve yourself, you just give up.

There is no spell that gives you discipline and willpower, and it is best that you just cut out the intermediaries here. Like motivation, willpower and discipline are nothing more than descriptors that are synonymous with "committed action."

You need to engage yourself with ACTION and nothing more. You are motivated, disciplined, and willful in your endeavors when you are committed to acting on your values, which are required to achieve your goals, even when you do not feel like following the path to an engaged life full of rewards.

Learn to act consistently on your values no matter how you feel, and once it becomes a bona fide habit, THEN you feel like you have willpower and discipline. Your mind will constantly figure out ways to avoid leaving your comfort zone and engaging in life to the fullest. Do not be fooled by all of the stuff in the middle. Head straight to your values.

Day 19:
When Confidence Escapes You

"Each time we face our fear, we gain strength, courage, and confidence in the doing."

Theodore Roosevelt

If you continue to wait for the feelings of confidence before you start daring to adventure, you will be forever in waiting. Remember, confidence comes after practice.

Embark on your GRAND ADVENTURE in a mindful way, with your values as a guide. You now have all the tools to do these things, and you understand the main reasons for low self-confidence and how to defuse all of them.

A refresher is below:

- You correct excessive expectations by unlatching yourself from all perfectionist demands and engage fully in the challenging task.

- You correct harsh self-judgment by unlatching yourself from mind's commentary on your performance and engage fully in the challenging task.

- You correct your preoccupation with fear by unlatching yourself from your stories of failure and rejection, and engage fully in the challenging task.

- You correct your lack of experience by committing to your values and through committed action. You gain experience by stepping out of your comfort zones and practicing.

- You correct your lack of skills by committing to your values and committed action.

You follow values such as persistence and dedication, and you make room inside of yourself for the discomfort involved, which could be anything from boredom or frustration to anxiety or fear. Physical pain might even be involved.

Do what you need to do to improve your skills, and ensure that are working on the right skills, the ones that really make a difference. Many athletes and businesspeople fool themselves because they work hard at the skills that come to them easily; yet, they avoid exercising the challenging skills that would take them to the next level. Do not be that person.

Remember, accept your thoughts and feelings, choose a valued direction, and take action mindfully. There is no spell that you can cast; there is only the matter of trusting you values regardless of how you feel and relying on yourself to do what matters even if you feel discomfort and terror.

Day 20:
Peak Performance

"I know the price of success: dedication, hard work and an unremitting devotion to the things you want to see happen."

Frank Lloyd Wright

When our focus is genuinely narrowed, we find ourselves in "the zone;" time stops and there is no self-consciousness or any form of commentary from inside of us about our performance. Nothing distracts us because our attention is completely on the task, and all the skills you have practiced come together in a fluid way, so that the actions of your body and mind seem effortless.

This is the state of peak performance.

There are three phases to peak performance that you can find in the book *The Psychology of Enhancing Human Performance* by psychologists Frank Gardner and Zella Moore. Each phase is crucial to your evolution to solid self-confidence.

The book details the following:

- Pre-performance phase

- Performance phase

- Post-performance phase

Let us look at all three.

Pre-Performance Phase

The pre-performance phase is about preparation. It involves training and practice. This is the where we read literature, train, and practice our essential skills, including mindfulness. You will call repeatedly upon your values, especially self-development and persistence, defuse from all the reasons telling you not to practice, make room for the discomfort that involves fears and anxieties, and engage fully in practicing the skills you need to become self-confident in the activity.

Performance Phase

The performance phase is where you put all of your preparation and hard work together. You apply the skills in an effective way within the performance situation. The key is task-focused attention. In other words, you focus your attention on the essential details in order to do the task well.

Your spotlight needs to shine upon what is relevant for success. All other things are left in the dark or dim lights, and they include thoughts about your appearance, what others might be thinking, your movements and limb placement, the outcome of the activity, what happened 10 minutes ago, what you could be doing better, or the mistakes that you have made. You do not think about how others will judge you and your performance or that you are screwing everything up. Any thoughts that are negative, positive, presumptuous, or true do nothing to assist your performance. They do nothing more than distract you from the activity.

However, knowing this will not stop the thoughts from arriving. If you start challenging the thoughts, attempt to forcefully push them away, or recite affirmations to instill confidence, you create further distractions instead of focusing attention on the task. Instead, you use your mindfulness skills as you defuse yourself from unhelpful thoughts, expand around difficult feelings, and engage fully in the relevant aspects of the experience. The greater your ability to do this, the better your performance will be, and eventually you will be so good at it, you hit "the zone."

Post-Performance Phase

The way in which you respond after your performance is as important as what happens pre-performance and during it. Regardless of how good or bad you did during the performance, the healthiest response is to reflect mindfully upon it, and learn and grow from the experience.

Bring openness and curiosity into this phase as you look to find out what worked, what did not work, and what can we do differently the next time. On the other hand, if you are happy with your performance, congratulate yourself for all the hard work that it took to get into this position. However, do not allow positive thoughts to linger because you do not want to fuse to any idea that you are "the best." They are a distraction as well, and remember to stay in the moment.

If your performance was below expectations, then practice self-acceptance and defuse from any harsh self-judgments. Speak to yourself with kind words and realign with your values. Furthermore, commit to evolving from the experience based on what you have learned.

Finally, actively appreciate yourself. Appreciate your devotion to become a better person, your willingness to take risks, and the things you did right. Use the appreciation to fuel you, so that you continue to drive ahead with enthusiasm, and remember that the more actions of confidence that you take, the closer you get to really being confident.

Day 21:
Healthy Balance

"We need to introduce a little balance into our life. Part of this balance means not missing out on some of the marvels of life around you, the fun, some excitement, or other challenges in life."

Catherine Pulsifer

In the 2008 U.S. Open, golfer Tiger Woods' experienced pain in his left knee after having arthroscopic surgery on two separate occasions. Despite the pain, he won the tournament. Another competitor in the tournament, Kenny Perry, commented that Woods "beat everybody on one leg."

During the event, Woods focused on the task and it took him far from his pounding knee during every shot he took for four straight days.

While everyone applauded his efforts, you have to ask the questions: Did he do the right thing by continuing through the tournament on an aching knee? Did he risk further injury or long-term health by going into "the zone" instead of going to the emergency room?

We must confess, there is a dark side to "focus" and "engagement." We can become so caught up in achieving our goals that we fail to pay attention to our minds and bodies. Sometimes, if we dedicate ourselves to achievements, we give up a lot, and eventually fall hard. We crash into a state of depression, suffer from stress-related ailments like high blood pressure, or substance abuse finds us.

It happens all of the time. High achievers become so focused on their tasks that they neglect their health and well-being, and over time it leads to burnout, injury, or illness. It can also lead to divorce and broken families. To sustain peak performance over the long haul, you have to look after your health and well-being, as well as your relationships.

Make no mistake, excellence requires sacrifice. To be good at anything, that thing has to be a priority, and you have to devote time, energy, and effort as you search for self-confidence and beyond. However, you must be smart about what you sacrifice. There are things you can give up, like social media, happy hours at the bar, or binge-watching mindless television shows, but you do not sacrifice spending quality time with our kids, and you do not give up date night with your beloved partner.

Many of us, probably most of us, find fulfillment in being competent at professional and personal tasks while maintaining a balanced and rewarding life outside of those tasks. However, many people want to be more than "competent." They want to reach to the highest level. When you get to this place, you understand that significant sacrifice over a long amount of time is required. Therefore, you must give up things to get there, and it is a challenge to remove things that have been a part of our lives to make room for more important things.

The challenge we face is finding balance between personal relationships and family, work, and recreation, while also staying mindful of our physical and mental health and well-being. It is hard to get it perfectly right, so we must fine-tune it on a regular basis. Once a week, take 15 minutes to reflect honestly on your balance between the loving people in your life, you work, your leisure activities, and your health. The essential element we are looking for here, as has been the case throughout the book is the question, "Are you living by your values in every area of your life?" Can you improve or adjust a few things to create more balance? You probably can, and should.

Good luck with finding the balance of life. It is yet another key to your evolution and your newfound confidence.

www.ingramcontent.com/pod-product-compliance
Lightning Source LLC
Chambersburg PA
CBHW051909250726
48659CB00002B/562